Let's Count to

100!

Let's Count to
100!

Masayuki Sebe

SCHOLASTIC INC.
New York Toronto London Auckland
Sydney Mexico City New Delhi Hong Kong

There are 100 mice!
Count them all, starting with the brown ones.

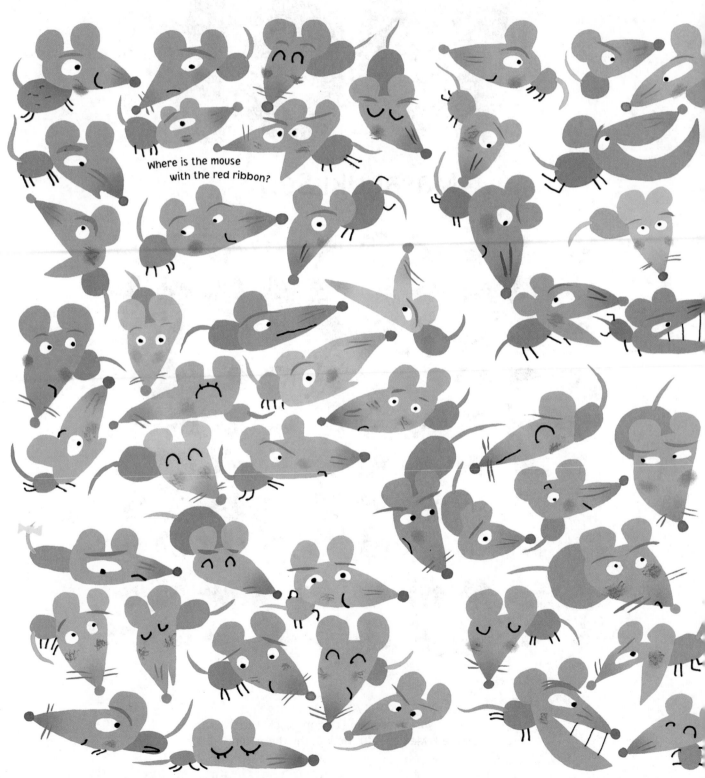

Where is the mouse with the red ribbon?

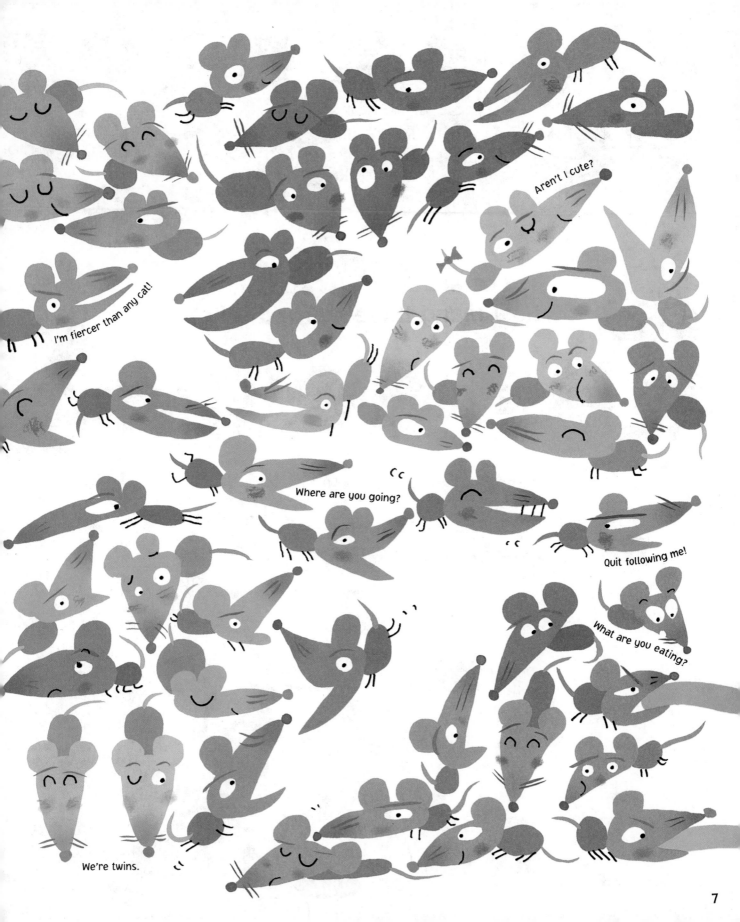

There are **100** cats!
How many have striped tails?

Please don't pull my whiskers.

Gotcha!

Hee! That tickles!

How many cats are in my family?

Who are you?

Have you seen the ladybug?

9

There are **100** moles.

What's that?

I don't want to know!

You stink!

Pee-ew!

Ahh! I feel much better.

I'm digging.

Careful!

10

How many are snuggled up with a frog?

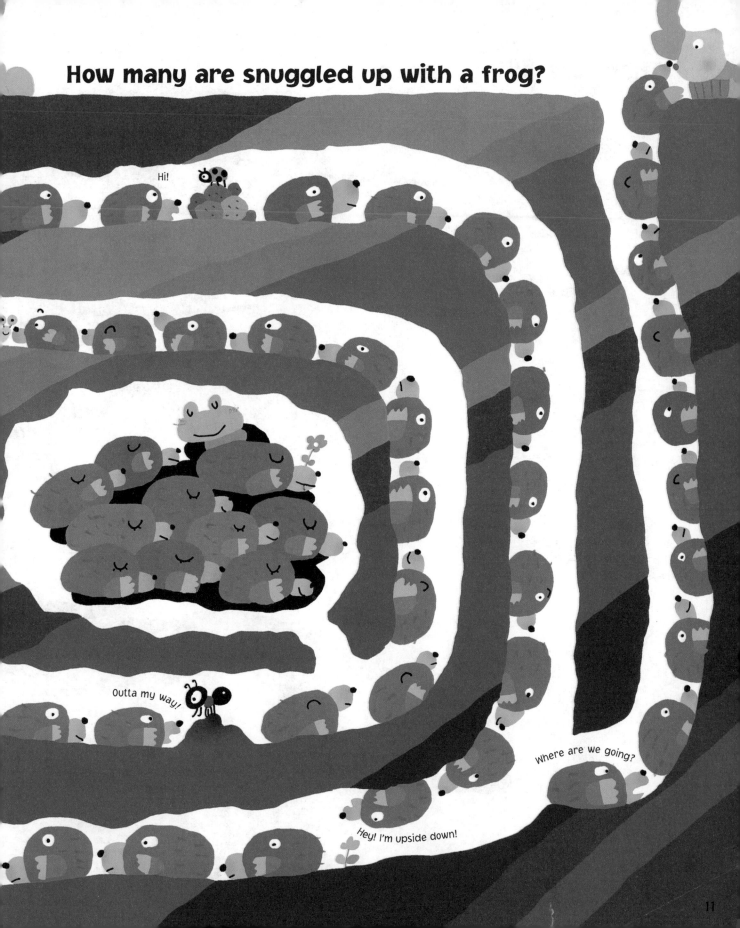

There are **100** sheep ...

and 1 rabbit! (Do you see him?)

There are **100** birds.

Are there enough berries for everyone?

Yum!

I like being upside down.

Got it!

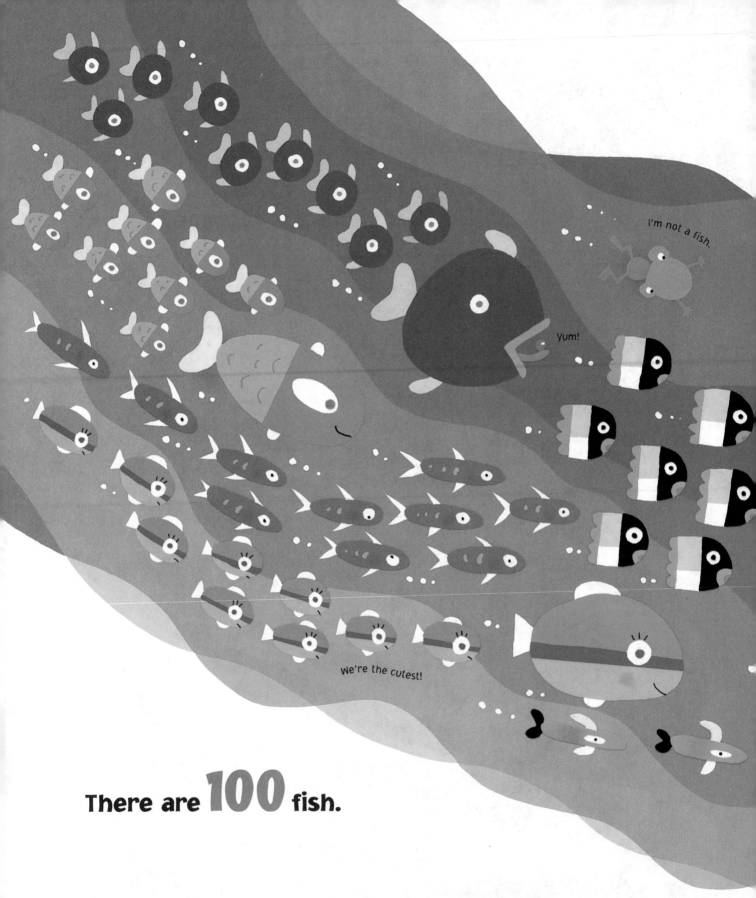

There are **100** fish.

How many different kinds of fish are there?

There are **100** elephants!

I need to cool off.

That hurt!

How many elephants are sleeping?

How many elephants are smiling?

I'm lost.

Ready, set, count!

That looks tasty!

There are **100** kids!

Count them all.

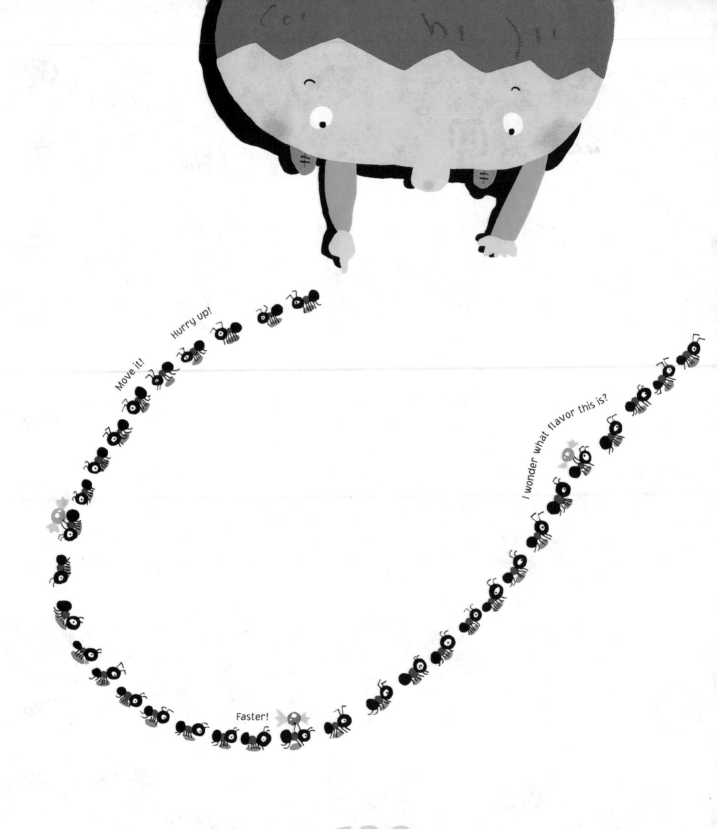

There are **100** ants!

How many are carrying candy?

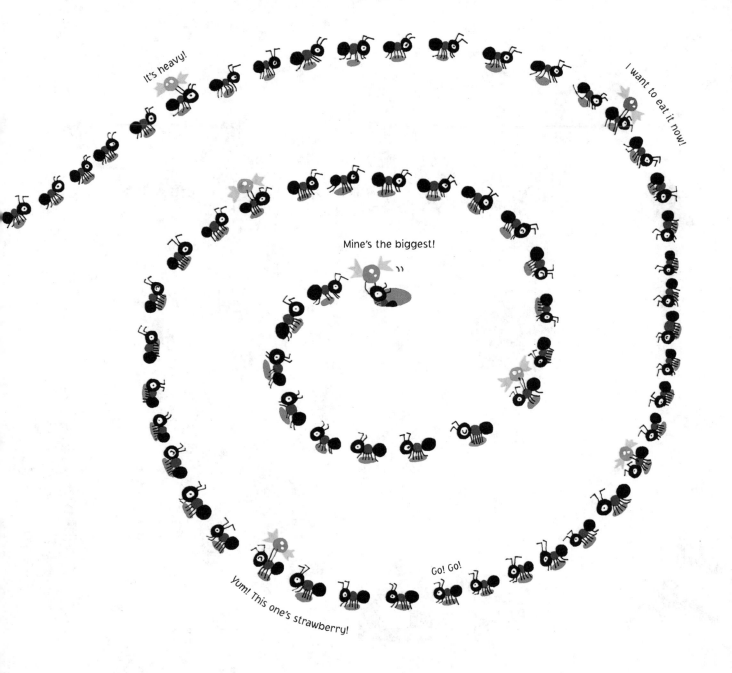

I want a carrot.

Maybe I should play outside.

Where is the mouse?

24

There are **100** cars and trucks!

Beep! Beep!

Woop-woop!

Wee-oo! Wee-oo!

I like watermelon.

And **100** houses!

There are 10 mice, 10 cats, 10 moles, 10 sheep, 10 birds, 10 fish, 10 elephants, 10 kids, 10 ants and 10 houses.

What?

That makes **100** in all!

Tweet!
Tweet!

Meow!

Yikes — a cat!

Go! Go! Go!

Did you see ...

the mouse with the
yellow bow?
(pages 6-7)

this cat?
(pages 8-9)

the farting mole?
(pages 10-11)

the snowman?
(pages 12-13)

this bird?
(pages 14-15)

this frog?
(pages 16-17)

the elephant
holding a pineapple?
(pages 18-19)

who was wearing
this hat?
(pages 20-21)

the girl with a
strawberry on her head?
(pages 20-21)

the boy cuddling this
cat?
(pages 20-21)

this sleeping ant?
(pages 22-23)

the mouse's house?
(pages 24-25)

this house?
(pages 24-25)

this truck?
(pages 24-25)

Originally published in Japanese under the title *Kazoetegoran Zembu de 100*
by Kasei-sha Publishing Co., Ltd.
English translation rights arranged through Japan Foreign-Rights Centre

ISBN 978-0-545-41532-3

12 11 10 9 8 7 6 5 4 3 2   12 13 14 15 16 17/0

Printed in the U.S.A.   40

First Scholastic printing, January 2012

English edition edited by Yvette Ghione